The Universe Will Give You Flores

Darlene Moreno

PUBLISHING

The Universe Will Give You Flores
© 2024 Darlene Moreno

All rights reserved. No part of this book may be reproduced, distributed, or transmitted in any form or by any means, including photocopying, recording, or other electronic or mechanical methods, without the prior written permission of the publisher, except in the case of brief quotations embodied in critical reviews and certain other noncommercial uses permitted by copyright law.

For permission requests, write to the publisher, addressed "Attention: Permissions Coordinator," at the e-mail address below.

davina@alegriamagazine.com

Illustration by Manuela Guillén

ISBN: 9798991125017

Library of Congress Control Number: 2024919318

Published by Alegria Publishing

Dedico esta colección de poesía a mi mami:
tú me enseñaste a luchar en esta vida.

And to little Darlene:
you wanted to be a poet;
you always were.

PREFACE

"Ya no quiero que llores,
the universe is gonna give you muchas flores."
– "A letter to my younger self" by Ambar Lucid

I still think of little Darlene crying in her Wilmington bedroom in Los Angeles, writing poetry. I was 14 years old, and I had just lost my mom to cancer. Everyone in the family was preoccupied with themselves, with their own grief. I was lost in grief too, questioning my place in this world after just losing my first home: my mami.

Growing up in my hometown was also challenging; I constantly felt misunderstood and alone, and I saw little promise of a vibrant future, knowing one typically needed to leave to find better opportunities.

When life got difficult, I retreated to what offered me solace and sanctuary: books and poetry. I read so many fictional books that transported me to places I could only dream of, places far away from home. Writing, a passion I'd discovered in the first grade, became my outlet for processing life around me. I remember crafting verses about flowers and a whimsical little poem about gum stuck to the bottom of my shoe. Writing became my medicine, but it was also a means to escape. As I grew up, I gradually learned how to embrace my reality. I couldn't envision then how my life would unfold.

What originally started as a quest for home and love outside of myself, and a desire to break free from my hometown, transformed into a journey of connection, discovery, and storytelling. Life unfurled through heartbreak, rejection, loss, triumph, joy, and adventure.

My worldview expanded drastically when I studied abroad in Lyon, France and volunteered in a small village in Armenia in my early twenties, where a loving family embraced me as their own.

Navigating adulthood in Glendale and Hollywood also broadened my perspective, as did my experience with breast cancer at 26, which brought an intimate encounter with physical pain and a pivotal moment to reflect on my life's trajectory.

I especially reflected about the kind of impact I wanted to have in the world. I recalled teenage dreams of politics and diplomacy— yearning for influence— which stemmed from childhood powerlessness. Understanding this desire led me back to myself, to that little 10-year-old girl who did community service out of love for the people in her neighborhood. I learned that true power grows within the heart.

Now in my 30s, spiritual introspection and community-building nurture my soul. I am engaged in a collective of Latinx/e artists preserving our family narratives and cultures, which sparked the creation of this book. I contribute to transnational feminist communities, advocating passionately for various causes while fostering communities of care. Along the way, I also learned to advocate for myself.

This poetry collection has proved a necessary and tumultuous return to self. Many of us in our healing journeys refer to this shedding and renewal process as "unlearning" or "re-parenting;" for me, it has also been about "replanting," offering myself the opportunity to lead a healthier, more heart-led existence in México.

Now, here in Ciudad México, my latest home, I continue to forge connections with my family, my culture, and myself. I've come to accept that "home," isn't a permanent place, but a harbor where I feel safe, cherished, and sustained, even in transience. Home is a deep rootedness in my values: truth, liberation, justice for the oppressed, love as an everflowing source, and reverence for my own sacred journey. I am home.

This book is a gift to every Darlene I have been and a promise to all the Darlenes I will become. Here's to becoming my own muse and to cultivating a haven for my tears to water this field of self-love.

As long as I show up whole-hearted, vulnerable, and ready for the wind to take me where it may - be it heartbreak, confusion, pain, or moments of solitude - I trust the universe will continue to give me flores, like so:

Table of Contents

The universe will plant you in soil

It's Time	12
Inheritance	13
Dolores	15
Hierbabuena	17
Books	19
Self-Parenting	21
Abandonment	22
Salt	23
I Should Have Known	25
Zenith	26
I Say I'm Not a Poet	27
The C Word	29
What Happens After Cancer?	32

The universe will gift you water

Restless	34
Witnessed	36
Overflow	37
Why Did God Make Mountains?	38
Popocatépetl	39
Maneras	40
Sweat	41
Paris, in Like	42
Repiqueteo	44
Tren al corazón	46
Llorar	48
Cempazuchitl	49

The universe will illuminate your path

Immigrant Mothers	52
An Immigrant's Grief	53
I Met a Man Today	54
Decolonization	55
Temazcal	57
To México, con amor	58
Dear Lilit	60
Tatik	62
The Ring from Vernissage	64
Gaza	65
A Response to Noor Hindi	66
Advocacy	67
Protest	68
Community Warriors	70
The Revolution Will Come	71

The universe will help you bloom

The Magic Lives in Me	74
¿A dónde pertenezco?	75
Pan y chocolate	76
Yo soy	78
Perséfone	79
Coyoacán	80
Orquídea	82
Jacarandas	83
Acknowledgements	87
About the Author	89
About the Artist	91
Spotify Playlist	93
Nourishing Creativity	95

The universe will plant you in soil

IT'S TIME

It has become impossible to escape myself any longer, to ignore my body filled with echoing questions and metastasizing grief. There is nothing left to do but to write until the words flood into the ground. Write until they wash away the fears and the withering petals. Write until they nourish to life new flowers.

INHERITANCE

From my mother,
I inherited my love of lipstick,
the color of a mirasol pepper,
that she would paint on her lips
in the car before heading inside
to her doctors' appointments.

The way her deep-belly laughs
made her body tremble,
the sound resonating through walls
letting you know she was
more than just existing–
She was alive.

From my mother, I inherited the way she
turned strangers into friends
and friends into family.
She built bridges between people
and taught me to build my own table and chairs
if they were not already made.

From my mother, I inherited her curiosity
for the world, an immigrant woman who
walked on foot to a new country,
who let accent and desire escape from her lips,
breathing new life wherever she went.
She learned as much as she could

about anything and everything.
Nada la detenía. Because of her,
I cultivated an adoration of Spanish love songs
and stories of the magic that moves us.
Eyes closed, head swaying, she would say,

Darlene Moreno

Yo estoy enamorada del amor,

I am in love with love itself.
Or atleast, the idea of it. From my mother,
I also inherited the desire
to be with someone just to have them.
Cycles of heartbreak and pain,
and impressionable romances.

Insecurities the size of seas
and misplaced boundaries,
maybe too trusting,
maybe too hopeful,
maybe staying too damn long
in places not meant for us.

After years of giving
herself to people,
she left herself only crumbs
until there was nothing,
until the cancer grew,
until she was no more.

From my mother,
I also inherited the cancer that took her life,
when it returned years later
trying to tie up loose ends,
trying to find a home in my body.
It was a battle I would not lose.

Because I am my mother's daughter
with an obstinate will
and fighting spirit
that I inherited from her too.

DOLORES

My heart broke once when you left
and again when I realized that the world

kept spinning on without you–
the vecino gets in their car and drives to their job,

the bills keep coming and clutter the kitchen table,
the mercados are crowded and the lines are long.

I walk around, popping garbanzos in my mouth
like you did in the store as we grazed the aisles.

A gardener arrives to cut the grass.
Your roses have wilted; they cried for you too.

The traffic on the 110 hasn't moved
and makes sure I'm late to wherever I'm going,

as if I know where I'm going.
I've driven these same streets for decades

searching for you. In my dreams, I knock
on every door, asking, *Have you seen my mother?*

Have you seen my mother?
Mami, maybe you thought that the world

would tear you from our hearts,
but how could it? When I hear your voice

in every rush of wind, your laughter in every chiste,
your love in every song, and your grief

with every interlocking gaze in a señora's face.
I still see you sitting on the front porch,

waiting with sandía in one hand
and a phone in the other,

announcing to your comadres,
La Darlene ya llegó de la escuela.

How could I forget you?

Your body gave me life,
and it also gave me pain.

Dolores.

Dolor. Sufrimiento.
Your middle name.

Dolores.

Was I also born to live through such pain?

Dolores.

Maybe if I had said your name three times,
you could have stayed with me forever.

HIERBABUENA

Hierbabuena.
Hierba mala.
¿Cúal hierba me curará mañana?

Hierbabuena es la que recuerdo al comer
las albóndigas que mi mamá preparaba,
sus manos formaban bolitas de carne
los días en los que me sentía enferma.
El aroma de las zanahorias, las papas y las calabacitas
me alimentaban con una tortilla enrollada,
y su caldo, me devolvía la vida.
Mi mamá, me apapachaba
y me cantaba: "sana, sana, colita de rana,
si no sanas hoy, sanarás mañana".

Hierba mala es la que aprendí a tomar en mi niñez
cuando mis hermanas me decían
que era demasiado emocional,
demasiado dramática,
demasiado inestable,
demasiado,
demasiado,
demasiado...
Yo tomaba ese trago amargo sin pensar,
mientras lentamente ingresaba a mi estómago
y dejaba que mi cuerpo lo absorbiera.
No sabía cómo distinguir lo que era mío
y lo que era de otra persona.

Hierbabuena.
Hierba mala.
¿Cuál hierba me curará mañana?

En la madurez aprendí que el poder ya no queda
en manos de otras personas,
como adulta me puedo preparar mis propios alimentos,
y yo escojo tomar un té de hierbabuena,
caliente y reconfortante,
calmante y sustancioso.

Y aunque mi mamá ya no está,
yo he aprendido a beber
solo lo que me fortalece.

BOOKS

Mami held my hand as I skipped on concrete,
pretending that the gray sky was dyed cotton candy
instead of pollution from the oil refineries.
I was 8 years old when I knew mami was sick,

and that a lot of our neighbors were too.
Life here was full of many ailments and hardships,
and the only thing that made the worry melt away were
our anticipated trips to the library.

At arrival, any gloom would stay at the door
and inside that building, I saw only possibility.
There was no place like the library,
where I met wizards and visited islands of blue dolphins,

where I read about high school crushes in teen books
and heroines who were mediums, vampires, and princesses.
There I found my love of poetry in Robert Frost
and had *a lover's quarrel with the world.*

These stories left imprints as I held every word in my gaze,
sifting through whole worlds in the form of used pages.
I will chase that feeling for the rest of my life,
remembering how my happiest days as a child

were spent cross-legged on musty floors
with mami sitting next to me with headphones on
listening to English language tapes
in a place that felt more like home than home.

Reading these books fed my soul
in order to survive mami's cancer,
feeling misunderstood by my sisters

and treated like a nuisance by my father.

Eventually I learned to carry
what I learned in books as armor.
I felt protected, not by pirates or weapons,
but by my curiosity, hope, and soft heart.

Every step outside the library door
was one back into the real world,
and in my imagination's eye, I saw the sky more rosy
than gray with every book I read.

SELF-PARENTING

I started telling myself all the things I waited too long for papi to say:

You are kind.
You are valuable.
You are loved as you are.

ABANDONMENT

The biggest rejection was not by an old lover;
it was every single time I abandoned myself.

SALT

I loved you like table salt,
carelessly thrown on my food.
I marinated in your calculated eyes,
in your firm but anguished, hands,

in your charming voice. Every muddled morning,
I'd startle at the first sip of coffee,
tasting coarse salt, having mistook it for sugar.
I would find myself sick and trembling

when I consumed too much of you,
when I consumed too little of you,
when I consumed you at all.
I bathed myself in bath salt,

thinking it would heal this feeling,
but instead, it seared my skin
and left me wounded.
I waited until it stung,

until the ache of emptiness echoed through me
and the roses on my skin began to decay.
Then I sank in pink himalayan salt,
my blessed exorcism,

to purge me of you,
of your promises,
of your deceitful kisses,
of your deceptive touch.

Slowly, my body began to recalibrate,
sweating and shaking you out of my heart,
out of my psyche,

out of every pore.

Until I didn't recognize you anymore.
Until I began to recognize myself again.

I SHOULD HAVE KNOWN

I was an impeccable masochist
who used to seek you for pain
when I craved heartbreak
just to feel alive.

I wanted you to squeeze me like a pomegranate,
run my seeds into the ground,
and I secretly hoped that, one day,
they would bloom into something beautiful:

branches of red pearls like hanging hearts
ready for you to pluck.
I should have known better–
that fruit doesn't grow in rotten soil,

and not all things are worth waiting for.
You wanted to come and go as you pleased,
and I was taught that my role was to nurture
no matter the cost. Until it cost all of me.

I *should* have known better–
that I would not find what I was looking for
in thorn-ridden beds or in fruitless plans
or when disguised as desire.

I should have known better
that you could not fill me.
I was confused and enamored,
dazzled and willful, but never empty.

I should have known *better*–
that my desire for you was
actually hunger for myself.

ZENITH

It started not so long ago,
this new fear of heights.
I grip the railing until my knuckles turn white.

On the 23rd floor,
I make the sign of the cross.
Every time I arrive at my seat on an airplane,

I pray that I don't fall from the sky
and become an angel too soon.
Lord knows I know too many.

I have spent many nights
asking *What is this newfound fear?*
Where did it come from?

A desire to throw myself into the void?
Or maybe it's the memories running through my body,
of all the tumultuous highs of being with you.

I SAY I'M NOT A POET

Because my tongue is not sharp.
It is the shape of a shovel,
always digging for more
but never finding gold.

Because I learned in my childhood
(a long time ago) to only fit in tight spaces
and always ask for permission
and never, ever trust anyone,

not even myself. Because poetry is only writing
about love and heartbreak
and how my world was turned upside down
or rightside up. Or how someone's taste

lingers on my lips and
how my body broils when they're around.
And I? Baby, at night my bed sheets
feel more crisp without anyone in them.

Because if I say I'm a poet,
you, the audience, will expect me to perform,
for me to roll open the mat
and make you tea and invite you to stay.

And you will sit there with me,
waiting for my words to sound like prayers,
but instead, they are desperate pleas.
What will you think of me?

Because by now, I thought I had learned
how to peel every experience with grace

and bake them into poems full of wisdom
instead of my pain.

But in the years that
poetry fed me,
I also learned
to nourish myself.

Because I was not born a poet,
though through tribulations and struggles,
my solitude and my troubles,
a poet was born in me.

THE C WORD

It's the way people look at me with concern,
when they *know*. Compulsive stares
trying to catch if chunks of hair
will fall out at any moment.

They scan for scarlet surgery scars
that may conceal trauma
or purple punctures in my arms
that may conceal pain.

The whole experience is a circus,
and they are the spectators,
eyes clinically glued to me
as if I were a plague.

I'm not contagious;
you can't breathe this in.
They turn to me as if to say,
How careless; how did this happen?

As if I allowed for this to happen.
They cast a glare at my chest
to see if it looks any different.
It could have been worse.

Thank you for the reminder
that I could have died sooner,
that my own cells tried to kill me.
What can I say? What should I say?

Darlene Moreno

Fuck cancer
and my post-surgery catatonic stares,
crying for the aches to ease,
sliced open like butcher's meat.

My breasts were cut clean from my body,
an offering to the gods, my plea for life,
only to get filled with other parts of me.
I am my own Frankenstein's monster.

Fuck cancer.
When years later,
no matter the treatments
or gratitude, this body doesn't indulge

in food in the same way.
Doesn't dance or make love
the same way.
My body will never be the same.

Fuck cancer.
And how it tried
to narrate my days and nights
since childhood when it took my mother's life,

when it is the real imposter.
How it tried and failed.
It will no longer command
how I feel about myself.

This body is a work of art,
rough but malleable clay.

The Universe Will Give You Flores

No matter how many times
it has been distorted, contorted,

pierced, and sewn back together,
it has walked me through the fires
of cancer. I am no longer afraid
to call it what it is.

It can course its way through my body,
but it will never capture my tongue.

WHAT HAPPENS AFTER CANCER?

How do I live without
    pain
        loss
            sickness?

All I know is
    struggle
        darkness
            disappointment.

How do I learn
    to
        live
            again?

The Universe Will Give You Flores

The universe will gift you water

RESTLESS

As in I
rest less.
Rumpled bed sheets,
shallow breathing,
clenched fists–

I haven't slept in months.

Every night I cleanse my room with palo santo,
sifting smoke in counterclockwise circles,
waiting for the ghosts to leave
until I realize that there is no one there.
It's just me.

Me in a knot of anxiety,

worried about all the human things.
All the work things,
the love things,
the family things,
the will-I-ever-be-good-enough things, the

there's-gotta-be-more-to-life-than-how-I'm-living-now things.

So, so many things.
I lie awake listing all the ways
I want to show up tomorrow.
I start a catalog of all the ways
I got it wrong today.

I etch tallies on my arm

of every time my family
made me feel small,
of every sanctified rejection,
of every who-do-you-think-you-are?
With every turn in my bed,

I replay all the times I almost had it.

Like when I almost got the job
or when he almost liked me back
or when I almost said the right thing.
They say the opposite of almost
is always, but what if it's actually *enough?*

What if enough was filling my own cup?

If enough was
life-took-me-in-a-splendid-new-direction
and I-have-found-family-in-unexpected-places?
What if enough did not mean *as much as*
but meant *just right?*

What if I am just the right amount of me?

What if just right
is the blessed smoke
that I've been waiting for
to soothe my restless body
as I finally fall asleep?

WITNESSED

All I want is to be really seen,
as one admires a bird of paradise
in all its unfurling, wingspread radiance.

OVERFLOW

I was taught to ask for little
and accept even less.

But baby, that is old shit.
Let it go.
Let yourself overflow.

WHY DID GOD MAKE MOUNTAINS?

Is
it to
remind us
how small we are?
How vast this world is?
Or how close we are to heaven?

POPOCATÉPETL

El Popocatépetl erupciona
con una explosion
que estremece hasta el forro de mi alma.

¡Dios mío!,
esta fuerza magnética
me deja hipnotizada.

Tú eres el volcán
y yo el suelo,
fluyes sobre mi superficie.

Ya no resisto más
y dejo que tu lava me consuma
hasta transformar mi tierra.

MANERAS

Contigo quiero explorar
todas las maneras de decir *te amo*.

SWEAT

I feel the sweat drip down my thighs / there is no air conditioning in this damn city / in summer, I am suddenly aware of my body / I take cold showers trying to relieve me of this heat / of my desire for you / your smoldering gaze / I lie on the bed wrapped in my towel / I can almost feel your fingertips on my skin / your sweat dripping on me like a popsicle on a summer day / trickling / shiny / new

Darlene Moreno

PARIS, IN LIKE

It was winter time in Paris,
but I could still see the ground,
and the sky was filled with string lights
from the Christmas market stands

bursting with food and cheery trinkets.
I walked around with vin chaud, hot wine, in one hand
and a nutella crêpe in the other.
You walked with your curly hair and outstretched arms,

balancing on cobblestone streets like a tightrope walker.
We were so young, and I was impressed by a French guy
who spoke with music on his lips, romance on his hips,
and made love to the city with his feet.

We sang at the top of our lungs on our way to your place.
We did not take the metro, but walked the whole way-
one, two, three hours- I don't recall;
I just knew that I was with you, and you were exciting.

Your apartment is where we cooked together,
watched TED Talks about the voyage of Spanish guitars,
and made love after one of your jazz shows,
or at least, we really appreciated each other.

I don't think we were in love, but your home is where you
gave me my first cup of matcha.
You showed me your Japanese kintsugi, broken pottery,
dust blue fragments glued back together.

You looked into my eyes and really saw me.
I had been with other guys before,

but in my mind, you were my first.
The first one who showed me that what I really longed for

was great banter, romance, and a kind heart.
The first one who showed me that I deserved softness
as much as anything else.
Through knowing you, I discovered more of myself,

became my own kintsugi, piecing together
broken parts from past relationships,
with infrangible memories I have
of Paris and you…

REPIQUETEO

El repiqueteo de la lluvia sobre la ventana
me recuerda a ti
y de la manera cómo llegaste a mi vida
como un torrente de agua

que vino de un día al otro
por medio de la coincidencia y aventura
decidimos de subirnos a un tren
con destino a un parque sovietico

Ahi nos sentamos
en un banco
tus ojos enfocados en un libro
y los míos enfocados en ti.

¿Como te explico
que he pensado en ti desde ese dia
cada noche por 7 años
y 9,721 kilómetros?

Te he cargado conmigo a todos lados
en cada calle
cada viaje
y en cada sustancia que he comido

Te he buscado
en los labios de otros
imaginándome cómo saben
los tuyos

El tiempo ha pasado y nuestra relación se ha transformado
en largos correos electrónicos
con tus preguntas sobre la vida
como *¿Qué significa amar?*

No se la respuesta pero te escribiré mil canciones de amor
y otros mil poemas en español
por el miedo de decirte lo que siento
sabiendo que tal vez no los entiendas

Siempre pienso en ti
sentada en mi ventanilla
mirando la lluvia
escuchando el repiqueteo de mi corazón.

TREN AL CORAZÓN

Tren al norte,
tren al sur,
tren al corazón.

Madrugadas con los ojos pesados,
brillan con el primer sorbo de un cafecito,
me lo tomo al ritmo de un río cercano
que veo en su esplendor a través de mi ventana.

Días viajando por pueblos verdes,
cada tren me lleva más cerca
a mi destino,
a la aventura,
o tal vez al amor,
pero definitivamente a mí misma.

Como venas circulando
con cada experiencia,
con cada explosión de alegría,
con cada frustración pequeña,
viajar es todas estas cosas juntas.

Tren al norte,
tren al sur,
tren al corazón.

Viajar son sueños realizándose,
ver seres queridos con lágrimas y emoción,
abrazos que no terminan,
probar nuevas comidas,
nuevos sabores hasta quedar satisfecha,
conocer nuevas personas y sus historias,
sus pesares y sus almas libres.

También, viajar es la incomodidad,
los taxis que nunca llegan,
las tardes sudando en largos caminos,
andar por calles empedradas,
y las noches con pies adoloridos
extrañando mi almohada.

Sin embargo, cada día aprendo algo nuevo,
una palabra en otro idioma,
una nueva calle,
un mensaje del universo traído con el viento.
Entonces una vez más
embarco ese tren.

Tren al norte,
tren al sur,
tren al corazón.

LLORAR

Lloro por todas las veces
que me dijeron *no llores, eso no sirve para nada.*

Si de verdad no sirve, ¿por qué los seres humanos lloramos?

Llorar es parte del proceso,
las lágrimas fertilizan la tierra profunda de mi corazón
para que salgan flores en lugar de destrucción.

La amapola del perdón,
la orquídea de la curiosidad,
la flor de la pasión y la resolución,
la flor de chocolate,
un cosmos de amor para mí misma.

Todo es sentir y llorar,
todo es llorar y sentir.
Sentir y llorar,
hasta crecer y sanar.

CEMPAZUCHITL

We talk about wilted flowers
as if they were not once filled with a garden's sacred song,
as if they did not learn to hold on for so long.

We all have to let go when it is time,
and may our journeys lead us there with love and grace.

Darlene Moreno

The universe will illuminate your path

IMMIGRANT MOTHERS

They are monarcas in the sky,
and when they give birth to you,
they birth a constellation of dreams.

AN IMMIGRANT'S GRIEF

It hits in small waves and other times in torrents. A canción de amor en la radio. A limited international aisle at the grocery store. The desire to say *buenos dias* on early morning walks. Hearing chisme through the dinner chatter. Driving down the 101 wishing to turn and head South instead. Thinking of loved ones before going to sleep. Deaths that happen through phone calls. A walk on the beach thinking about how much water there is between you and me. An imaginary border that tries to tell me where I belong.

It comes with every game of *What would I be doing there now?* and *What might have been if we had never left?* A desire to have cafécito every morning in a colorful mercado. Eating quesadillas de flor de calabaza on a stool in the street. Missing the drives through fields of coconut trees that my grandparents once planted. Swaying to cumbias with my family as we dance around the pool in the New Year. An innate longing for a place I've never lived in. My body calls for it.

I dream of being held by those mountains. Did they witness generations of my family come and go? Would they one day take me back? I sigh in a language that migrated an ocean but is the only one I know. With swollen eyes I struggle to find the words. There are none. An immigrant's grief might have been planted in my parents, but its branches have grown into me…

I MET A MAN TODAY

Working at a seafood restaurant in La Roma.
He had lived in Texas with his wife and kids
until one day ICE caught him
and deported him back.

He has been living here in Mexico City since then
and expressed how much he misses his family,
but he said with such fortitude that in this life
es lo que dios quiera.

It's that Mexican optimism
that I am in awe of.
It's *lo que dios quiera*
even in the hardest of times.

DECOLONIZATION

Who will I be after my journeys in México?
A país with complex identities,
with indigenous peoples that belong
to the mountains, the ocean, and the trees,
with no man-made lines to separate them from the soil.

Who will I be when I rectify that *maybe?*
I saw myself in Frida–
       mestiza
              dark-hair
                      fair skin.

–because I unknowingly identified with her,
though her brush strokes covered the truth,
painted over Tehuana culture
used as palatable nationalism.
Who will I be when I recognize

I was born in L.A., yet foreign to these lands? Native peoples
belonged here before these streets were named
       Santa Monica
            Verdugo
                Los Feliz.

Colonizer names. Inherited histories
that have become mine too.
Who will I be when the colonized part of myself
comes to terms with the settler in me,
and when they are no longer at odds?

Darlene Moreno

When the Spanish shamelessly rolls off of my tongue
and the war within me transforms to still waters,
    will my
        ancestors
            know peace?

TEMAZCAL

The roads in Tulum
are dark with líneas invisibles
surrounded by bicycles and motorcycles.
I drive with blind faith

as I wish for the roads to lead me where they may,
and that my heart fills with the love
and spirit that a sage and his son
teach me in a temazcal.

Eyes closed, I listen
to the laughter of the wind,
the chants of joy, the washing away
of fear through sweat and tears.

The stars gaze at me
lying down, wrapped in cobijas,
praying for the earth to heal me,
and that my body

may one day be whole
without the tears of history,
of the lost languages,
of the forgotten memories.

Of the questions that ask,
Did my ancestors pray in the same way?
Did they also conceive songs in the moment?
Did they recreate the mother's womb for warmth?

I will never know,
but my spirit
has released these
to the universe.

TO MÉXICO, CON AMOR

In my mind lives that winter we spent on the beach,
swimming with rainbow fishes in the sea,
sipping from pineapples and feeling the breeze,

us lying on Tulum's white sand,
staring at the night sky and
thinking about how small we are in the face of the universe.

Thousands of miles away now,
we write iMessages like mailed letters.
We spend our work days dreaming

of the smell of horses in the fields of Michoacán,
stopping for paletas in the town square,
taking pictures of the tias on the street

with streamers in mosaic tinctures in the background.
That is how you know you are in México.
We send photographs of primos dancing with gusto

and share videos of us singing to rancheras,
our hands clutching at our chests
as if shot with an arrow, wounded by love.

We laugh at the memories, like our fight in Coyoacán
when you said you did not understand
why we profess love for a green, white, and red flag

that was only created half a century ago by a Spanish man.
Our questions of identity and what makes us Mexican
fueling the fight. Is it, like my prima quotes, that a Mexican is

born wherever the hell they want to be?
Un mexicano nace donde se le da la gana.
We reminisce on where our last names come from,

the days we spent in bathing suits, basking in cenotes,
the drives we took from ancient empire to ancient empire,
the conversations with strangers at mercados,

the week quarantined in that apartment in Ciudad México.
I know these memories will live with us forever.
We will always have México,

and México will always have us.

Darlene Moreno

DEAR LILIT

I see the news and think of you–
three people dead here,
fourteen soldiers fallen there,
thousands displaced.

The Caucasus nearly forgotten by the masses,
no world power to end the bloodshed,
to comfort your shoulders
and bring your loved ones home

To be Armenian, I've learned,
is the battle to simply *just be,*
a torch carried through generations–
one which you're tired of carrying, I know–

so you decide to carry flowers instead.
You, Lilit, of the mountain people,
who pick leaves in Tavush* to boil for tea
and share them open heartedly with strangers like me.

You, the daydreamer,
who enjoys lying on grass
in the middle of Yerevan*
as you watch walkers pass.

You, the challenger of conventions,
who never throws the first stone
but always makes jewels
from the ones that are thrown.

People like you carry wisdom
in the palms of your hands. You are a miracle,
brazen and molted by ancestral lands.

The Universe Will Give You Flores

I can see it in your eyes

as you see past the bombs in the sky,
scarlet hues reminding you of love, not war,
and the stars rouse you awake as you explore
what it means to be human during difficult times.

No warfare can infiltrate your heart.
No fear can take your mind under siege.
And Ararat,* that beautiful mountain, is yours
because you will it to be.

*jan = Armenian term of endearment, like "dear"
*Tavush = region in Armenia
*Ararat = a volcanic mountain made up of two cones that is described in the Bible as the resting place for Noah's Ark

Darlene Moreno

TATIK

I knew I was home the moment I met her
in the hallway with mahogany dressers.
She stood white-haired and honey-eyed, a big smile;

she had been waiting for me, too.
The wrinkles on her face were maps of the life she had lived,
and her hands mirrored a labor of love for her family.

I can still see her cracking open walnuts on the sofa,
making lavash* in the tonir,*
serving coffee from the jazzve,*

picking vegetables from her garden,
snatching my face to give me pachikner.*
The love of a grandmother, of my Tatik.*

I remember her arched hands reaching
for soviet-era books with worn cases,
reflections of her travels as a young woman in the USSR

and vast knowledge of parts of the world
she had never even seen.
Her love of adventure was even more apparent

in her acceptance to host me,
a volunteer in her village,
a stranger, for two years.

Tatik would wait for me to come home
from work every single day. At the kitchen table,
we would tell stories, laugh, cry, and break lavash* together.

We comforted each other on our hardest days,
and on days when I needed it, she reminded me of
the woman in the mirror I'd forgotten.

The Universe Will Give You Flores

Deep down, I think we both knew we had met in a past life,
but in this life, we were raised in distant cultures,
our tongues swaying in different languages.

Somehow we managed to still find each other
in this tiny village in Armenia, in this lifetime,
and I'm positive we'll meet again in the next.

*Tatik = Armenian word for "grandma"
*lavash = Armenian bread
*tonir = Armenian for an outdoor oven in the ground
*jazzve = Armenian coffee pot
*pachikner = Armenian word for "kisses"

Darlene Moreno

THE RING FROM VERNISSAGE

I was born in the earth,
stoned to creation,
like the glimmer of life
siphoned from the sacred women

in the crypt of ancient churches.
Hollow. Holy. Wrapped in embrace
around your tender finger,
I lived in an outdoor market

next to brazen rugs
woven by centuries of love–
Noor.* Apricot trees. Fields
in which lie the low whistles

of travesty, rooted so deep
the genocide still tremors
in the land no matter how far
or how much time.

But this ground, through brilliance,
resistance, still creates
such beautiful gems,
like me.

*Vernissage = an open-air market in Yerevan, Armenia
*noor = Armenian for "pomegranate"

GAZA

I wish I could turn the bombs and bullets into magic dust, and for your olives to anoint every head with a crown of love instead.

Darlene Moreno

A RESPONSE TO NOOR HINDI'S "FUCK YOUR LECTURE ON CRAFT, MY PEOPLE ARE DYING"

You don't own the flowers,
because you *are them*.
Your children become daisies
one limb at a time.

I am American and my money
fuels bombs sent to kill your loved ones.
The more I read Al Jazeera,
the more these flowers turn to dust

in my very hands,
trickling through my fingers
like an endless hourglass.
The bodies pile.

You don't own the flowers
because you are nature herself.
Resilient, verdant like your olive trees.
Too much for this earth.

I promise to plant you everywhere,
for as long as I can. One day,
you will write about all the flowers
that grow across Palestine like you own them.

ADVOCACY

Advocating for yourself is an act of love.
Advocating for others is a labor of love
that holds a mirror to the world.

PROTEST

With determined footsteps, I walk into the wave of the crowd to the beat of the drum, scribbled marker poster board in hand. I made it an hour ago.

I hear the voice over the megaphone guiding our chants, moving us forward.

Liberty. Freedom. Here. Now.

I see the banners, the flags, the pain carried by every single person, ushering justice with every breath.

My feet carry me forward to the next avenue with tears streaming like rivers of wrath. I think of *them*. My screams echo the pain of the people. Maybe close to home. Maybe thousands of miles away.

Bomb. Blast. Bullet. Bloodshed.

How do we allow this to happen? How do we stay this committed in service of people and systems that cause death and destruction? How are we walking through life without our hearts completely shattered?

My feet stomp. I'm out of breath. How much longer… until the next light? Until freedom?

With sweat pouring down my face, I remember that we are not here as charity. We are allies of the people. Of struggle. Co-creators of hope. Of gilded dreams.

People power = people over systems of power. Always.

I look up and see that progress has taken us to the next intersection, another light, another weary breath, another refusal to dim my own humanity.

COMMUNITY WARRIORS

This is an ode to the ones who strive under
table-stacks of requests, rules, and red-tape,
drafting agendas for board members one hour
and building dialogue with las señoras in the next.

To the change-maker-organizer by day
and helping-mami-and-papi-organizer-at-home by night.
To those who make sure the community
has chocolate con pan at their meetings

and on their tables at home so the children have
what they need to grow whether hungry for food
or hungry for purpose. To the ones writing grants,
jumping through hoops, pleading with funders

to show our people are human enough
and worth investing in.
To the ones who attend city council meetings,
ready for battle. Who propose plans for a better tomorrow

through gritted teeth and tired eyes.
Who go home empty-handed
and wake up ready to do it again.
To the ones who lead their teams

with gold hoop earrings, who wear
bright red hair and lipstick that speaks of resistance,
bold and without fear because they've been through it all
and nothing scares them anymore.

THE REVOLUTION WILL COME

The revolution will not come
underneath television screen mumbles,
with clenched fists and sweaty palms before bed,
nor with all the best wishes in our heads.

It will not come with neutrality
without strategy,
not with empty calls for peace.
If peace is the outcome, what is the process?

The revolution will not come
with *I can't do anything about it*
and being unwilling
to use our voices.

It will not come with violent systems
built on bodies and blood,
nor will it come from any politician,
no matter how well-intentioned.

No, the revolution will not come that way.

The revolution will come when we understand
that people in power flaunt their egos
because they are afraid to
face their own deaths.

It will come when we realize
that we do not fear death itself
but how we inflict it
on each other.

Darlene Moreno

The revolution will come when we
heed the calls of each others'
overflowing jars of pain
and carry them as our own.

It will come when our imagination
is wider than the status quo
and when our chains become threads
linking us to this joint struggle.

It will come when, in the depths of this ground,
we raise ourselves with a profound love
for community, justice, and ourselves.
Don't we deserve better?

The revolution will come
when you plant love in your heart
and allow it to bloom.

The universe will help you bloom

THE MAGIC LIVES IN ME

I search for magic in the world, forgetting that I hold the universe in my own cells.

¿A DÓNDE PERTENEZCO?

He volado a muchos lugares
a tierras que en mi mente nunca había imaginado
y sobre mares majestuosos
que han cautivado mi alma

He volado sobre montañas
donde brotaron civilizaciones antiguas
donde una familia me acogió con sinceros abrazos,
recibiéndome como hija del viento

He volado a dimensiones donde el destino me ha llevado
a sanar esos dolores y heridas que han traspasado
de generación en generación,
heridas que mi madre cargó,
pero conmigo se cierra el círculo, yo las entrego a la tierra.

He volado entre vidas pasadas y presentes,
reencarnada con el mismo espíritu de siempre,
ese que profesa que a mí no me digan
que yo no soy de aquí ni de allá,
porque yo florezco en todas partes.

PAN Y CHOCOLATE

I want a love made out of
Mexican table chocolate
that you break piece by piece
and boil in milk,

swirl with a spoon made out of
paciencia y ternura, patience and softness,
with a rhythm essential for growth.

Stir in star anise for calmness,
clove for protection,
un poquito de chile ancho
for fiery worship,

and three cinnamon sticks for balance.
Leave to simmer for 32 minutes–
one minute for every year I've been alive.

I want a love made out of
the sugar and butter
in a carnation-colored pan dulce
with a blooming flour

to satisfy my appetite,
each bite sprinkling
magic dust into the air.

I want a love made out of
poetry dripping from plates and mugs
and into hearts and bodies, a love where
all the spicy, bitter, and sweet

live together in harmony
knowing they are whole and splendid
in all their phases of alchemy.

I want a meal,
that when consumed,
reminds me
that all this love

already resides inside
y es mi pan y chocolate
de cada dia.

YO SOY

Yo no soy mi padre, ni mis hermanas,
No soy el lugar en el que nací, ni su ambiente destructivo.
No soy los familiares que no me entienden.
No soy el espacio vacío que quedó cuando murió mi mamá.
No soy sus dolores ni sus pesares.
No soy mis ansiedades ni mis enfermedades.
No soy el cáncer que me quiso arrancar la vida,
ni los sentimientos de lástima de las personas que me rodean.
No soy mis pesadillas ni mis temores,
no soy todas las cosas que tal vez él desea.

Pero sí soy las cosas que deseo en mí,
soy las estrellas y el respiro,
soy el agua de la cascada,
soy la tierra donde crecen los girasoles,
soy el viento que se mueve por mi pecho.
Soy amor, luchadora, chingona.
Soy la tela del universo entrelazada en un ser humano,
y eso, nadie me lo quita.

PERSÉFONE

Eso es del diablo,
decía mi familia
de cualquier cosa
que no les gustaba.

Mi música,
la gente LGBTQ+,
las cosas espirituales,
todo lo que no era católico.

Me río de lo que pensarían ahora de mí,
la feminista, chingona,
cuir, antipatriota…
Veo a través de todas las mentiras.

No, mi amor:
Soy una diosa
y los diablos se arrodillan
a mis pies.

COYOACÁN

Eran las once de la noche cuando un taxista me recogió
para trasladarme de Cuauhtémoc a Coyoacán,
él me habló de su vida en Oaxaca,
de sus tíos a los que visita cada seis meses.
Dijo que sus hijos que viven en la Ciudad de México,
habló también de su esposa y la bondad en la misma frase.
Charlamos de inmigración y la responsabilidad que nosotros,
los que nacimos fuera del país,
tenemos de seguir nuestras costumbres,
aunque sea la buenas,
y quizá no las otras.

Por supuesto que tienes derecho de estar aquí, me dijo.

Yo que cada día me lo cuestionaba:
¿Cómo puedo amar un lugar sin cegarme de sus historias?
¿Cómo puedo querer un lugar y honrar su presente?
No vengo a destruir, ni tampoco de aprovecharme, lo juro.
No, todo México no me pertenece,
y no me permito actuar como las personas que vienen y
hacen lo que quieren.

Para mí, amar a México es todo,
las calles, los espacios, la música, la comida y la gente.
Mi alegría viene de saludar a los vecinos,
de admirar las casas de colores alineadas en la calle,
y hasta las historias de miedo como en *El Callejón del Aguacate.*

Amarlo es sentir la vibración de poetas
cuando me siento en la Fuente de los Coyotes,
disfrutar un chile relleno en un restaurante de los Viveros,
platicar en el mercado con los vendedores,

The Universe Will Give You Flores

Amarlo es saborear un vigilante
(pan de miel y limón de Pancracia) y comermelo al caminar.

Vivir es gozar,
gozar es vivir *aquí*.

Al vivir aquí siento que pertenezco,
más de aquí que de allá.
Por ahora es así, más no sé si este sentimiento permanecerá.

Son las 11:35 de la noche
y después de una larga conversación de taxi
hemos llegado aquí, a mi lindo Coyoacán.

ORQUÍDEA

Fuí una orquídea
que creció en Estados Unidos,
un país que me quitó
hasta dejarme seca,
sin ilusiones,
con el corazón roto
y mis hojas en el suelo.

Hoy he decidido florecer
en México,
rodeada de mi familia,
mi cultura,
y mis raices.
Estoy aprendiendo
a vivir de nuevo.

JACARANDAS

Los Ángeles:

> I'm drinking a coffee in Hollywood.
> Outside of the window,
> I see tiny fluorescent-purple bulbs
> lining the streets in the middle of April.
>
> These jacarandas migrated here
> just like my parents did
> when they came to Los Ángeles
> with barely anything to their names.
>
> They planted the seeds,
> and I learned how to water them.
> I washed away the fears
> carried by a child of immigrants.

Ciudad México:

> I'm sitting on a bench in Parqué México,
> gazing at the jacarandas–
> blooming, vibrant
> blushing violet.
>
> I learned that these jacarandas
> traveled in the luggage of a Japanese man
> who smuggled seeds
> from Peru.
>
> And here they blossomed,
> lining the streets with bouquets.
> *The immigrant dream.* These two cities
> are threads tied together

Darlene Moreno

with similar heartbeats,
like the jacarandas
tied by migration.
Ciudad México, Los Ángeles:

both are a part of me.
To be replanted
is a blessing.

The Universe Will Give You Flores

ACKNOWLEDGEMENTS

I have to start by thanking Davina Ferreira and *Alegria Publishing!* Davi, thank you for taking a chance on me and for honoring my process and pain when I had not written in nearly 10 years.

I'd like to also thank my editors, Paloma Alcantar and S. Salazar. You were with me in various ways through the process of this book, and I am so grateful to have your passion and expertise guide mi librito to where it is now.

To Karina and Estefania - your poetry and friendship inspired me on days I did not feel like writing!

To Manuela, my artist - thank you for meeting me in the design process with such grace. I am honored to have your beautiful illustration on the cover.

To my sister, Michelle - thank you for always being there for me, whether it is attending my poetry events, watching my silly improv shows, or taking me to the airport every time I decide to travel or move thousands of miles away. I love you.

Thank you to my dear friends, Susi and Monica, for embracing me as I am. Sus - the title of this book and finding the artist for my cover were possible because of you.

To Lilit and Khanoum - I wish everyone could see the world through your eyes.

Cindy Chau - thanks for helping me tap into my own magic!

To my FF baddies, Sophia, Cassie, and RJ - thank you for inviting me to The Feminist Front and for creating a community for us to fight for social justice together.

Gracias a mi tía Martha y a mi tío Ramón, por tratarme como a una hija y darme todo el amor que nunca creí merecer. De ustedes aprendí que siempre he sido merecedora.

I thank the universe for sending me to live in Armenia where I met my adopted Armenian grandmother. Tatik, my angel - you were poetry in human form. Thank you for coming into my life in such an unexpected way.

To Ani jan, you will always be a part of me.

A mi familia y mis amiges en México, gracias por recibirme con los brazos abiertos.

Mami: sé que nunca me abandonas, y eres la luz que me guía. Este mundo te separó de mí demasiado pronto, pero te veo en todas las flores, la luna y las estrellas.

And to you, the reader, who has picked up my book - I am so delighted and honored that my stories can now be yours, too.

ABOUT THE AUTHOR

Darlene Moreno is a queer Latinx/e writer, poet, and feminist organizer from Los Angeles, now residing in Ciudad México.

Her work delves into themes of identity, culture, and belonging, and is deeply shaped by her Mexican culture and the people she meets in her travels, especially in Armenia. Most notably, she shares personal experiences such as losing her mother to breast cancer and her own diagnosis.

Outside of writing, Darlene enjoys singing along to broadway musicals, performing improv, exploring spirituality, and cooking dishes with sazón and an abundance of love.

Follow Darlene on Instagram **@darlenexmoreno** and visit her website at **darlene-moreno.com.**

Darlene Moreno

ABOUT THE ARTIST

Manuela Guillén is a freelance painter, muralist, and digital illustrator currently living in Philadelphia, PA. Born in Miami to Cuban and Salvadorian immigrant parents, Manuela has always had a love for art.

She has collaborated with local, national, and global art organizations such as PangeaSeed, Mural Arts Philadelphia, Gender Justice Fund, and more. Her murals can be found in both the U.S. and México.

Inspired by plants, tropical colors, and her cultural upbringing, Manuela aims to bring awareness to art education, mental health, sociopolitical causes, and environmental issues. As an Art teacher, Manuela hopes to inspire her students to be creative as she continues to bring communities closer together through art.

You can find Manuela's art on Instagram **@lazybeamarte** and her website, **manuelaguillen.com.**

Darlene Moreno

The Universe Will Give You Flores

SPOTIFY PLAYLIST

(Scan this code with your Spotify app!)

Here is a list of Latinx/e songs and artists that sustained me throughout the process of writing this book. I hope you enjoy them!

"María La Curandera" - Natalia Lafourcade
"Sola" - Jessie Reyez
"A letter to my younger self" - Ambar Lucid
"Noche No Te Vayas" - Daphne Michelle
"Planeando El Tiempo" - Elsa y Elmar
"Hasta La Raíz" - Natalia Lafourcade
"No Necesito Más" - Marissa Mur
"Explotar Contigo" - TOURISTA
"Amor" - Alta Elegancia y Dannylux
"El baile y el salón" - Café Tacvba
"La Magia" - Little Jesus
"Versos de Placer" - maye
"amantes y amigos" - Elsa y Elmar
"Me Rehúso" - Daniel, Me Estas Matando y Reconversión
"Que Pecado" - Escarlata
"cigarrito y café" - Josue Alaniz y Carlos Colosio
"Crazy Love" - Irene Diaz
"Nunca Tristes (Me Vale Madre)" - RENEE
"Moody" - maye

Darlene Moreno

NOURISHING CREATIVITY

Here are all the cafés and restaurants that nourished me while I was writing this poetry collection.
Check them out!

Los Angeles
HOLLYWOOD
- Bolt - 5648 Hollywood Blvd
- Groundwork Coffee - 1501 N Cahuenga Blvd
- Hollywood Coffee House - 4972 Hollywood Blvd
- La Poubelle Bar & Bistro - 5907 Franklin Ave
- Sabor y Cultura - 5625 Hollywood Blvd
- The Oaks Gourmet Market & Cafe - 1915 N Bronson Av.
- The Sisters Cafe Vietnamese & Asian Fusion - 5910 Sunset Blvd Unit A

Ciudad México
COYOACÁN
- Café Negro - Centenario 16, Del Carmen
- Café Ruta de la Seda - Aurora 1, Del Carmen
- El Olvidado - Calle Pdte. Carranza 267, Santa Catarina
- Librería U-Tópicas - Felipe Carrillo Puerto 60, Coyoacán
- Marabunta - Miguel Ángel de Quevedo 485c, Romero de Terreros
- Pancracia - Tatavasco 17, Av. Francisco Sosa, Santa Catarina
- The Nest Coffee Bar - 04010, Santa Catarina

CUAUHTÉMOC
- Boicot Café - Jalapa 99, Roma Nte.
- Cafebrería El Péndulo - Álvaro Obregón 86, Roma Nte.
- Libertario Coffee Roasters - C. Orizaba 16, Roma Nte.
- Postales - Monterrey 177, Roma Nte.

Darlene Moreno